TO: 朗朗:

May the days ahead be filled with God's blessings and His unfailing love, as you continue to serve Him.

Congratulations on your Baptist !

FROM:

Aunt Aileen   4-14/2006

Real Questions...
Real Answers...

his
DEVOTIONAL

5 minutes
a Day
FOR TEENS

his
DEVOTIONAL

5 minutes a Day
FOR TEENS

The quoted ideas expressed in this book (but not scripture verses) are not, in all cases, exact quotations, as some have been edited for clarity and brevity. In all cases, the author has attempted to maintain the speaker's original intent. In some cases, quoted material for this book was obtained from secondary sources, primarily print media. While every effort was made to ensure the accuracy of these sources, the accuracy cannot be guaranteed. For additions, deletions, corrections or clarifications in future editions of this text, please write BRIGHTON BOOKS.

Scripture quotations are taken from:

The Holy Bible, King James Version

The Holy Bible, New International Version (NIV) Copyright © 1973, 1978, 1984, by International Bible Society. Used by permission of Zondervan Publishing House. All rights reserved.

The New American Standard Bible®, (NASB) Copyright © 1960, 1962, 1963, 1968, 1971, 1972, 1973, 1975, 1977, 1995 by The Lockman Foundation. Used by permission.

The Holy Bible, New King James Version (NKJV) Copyright © 1982 by Thomas Nelson, Inc. Used by permission.

Holy Bible, New Living Translation, (NLT) Copyright © 1996. Used by permission of Tyndale House Publishers, Inc., Wheaton, Illinois 60189. All rights reserved.

New Century Version®. (NCV) Copyright © 1987, 1988, 1991 by Word Publishing, a division of Thomas Nelson, Inc. All rights reserved. Used by permission.

The Message (MSG) This edition issued by contractual arrangement with NavPress, a division of The Navigators, U.S.A. Originally published by NavPress in English as THE MESSAGE: The Bible in Contemporary Language copyright 2002-2003 by Eugene Peterson. All rights reserved.

The Holman Christian Standard Bible™ (HCSB) Copyright © 1999, 2000, 2001 by Holman Bible Publishers. Used by permission.

Cover Design by Kim Russell / Wahoo Designs
Page Layout by Bart Dawson

ISBN 1-58334-235-4

TABLE OF CONTENTS

Introduction

Everybody knows you're a *very* busy guy. But here's a question: can you squeeze *five* little minutes into your hectic schedule? If you're a wise guy, the answer will be a resounding yes. Why? Because the five minutes in question are the minutes that you give to God!

God has a plan for everything, and that includes you. But figuring out that plan may not be easy. That's why you need to talk to God . . . *a lot*. The more you talk to your Creator, the sooner He will help you figure out exactly what plans He has in store for you. So do yourself a favor: Start talking to Him *now*. As you begin that conversation, this little book can help.

This book contains 31 short devotional readings of particular interest to guys who, like you, are very busy. Each chapter contains a Bible verse, a brief devotional reading, quotations from noted Christian men (plus quotes from a few women tossed in for good measure), and a prayer.

Would you like to have a life that's above and beyond the ordinary? Talk to God about it. Do you have questions that you can't answer? God has answers. Are you seeking to improve some aspect of your life? The Bible is the greatest self-improvement book of all time. Do you want to be a better person and a better Christian? If so, ask for God's help and ask for it many times each day . . . starting with a regular, heartfelt morning devotional. Even five minutes is enough time to change your day . . . and your life.

Five Minutes for God

Let the words of my mouth and the meditation of
my heart be acceptable in Your sight, O Lord,
my strength and my Redeemer.
Psalm 19:14 NKJV

*E*ach day has 1,440 minutes—can you give God five of them? Of course you can . . . and of course you should!

This book asks that you give your undivided attention to God for *at least* five minutes each day. And make no mistake about it: the emphasis in the previous sentence should be placed on the words "at least." In truth, you should give God lots more time than a measly five minutes, but hey, it's a start.

Has the busy pace of life here in the 21st-century robbed you of time with God? If so, it's time to reorder your priorities and your life. Nothing is more important than the time you spend with your Heavenly Father, so slow down and have a word or two with Him. Then, claim the peace and abundance that can be yours when you regularly spend time with your Heavenly Father. His peace is offered freely; it has been paid for in full; it is yours for the asking. So ask. And then share.

Thoughts for Today

Be still: pause and discover that God is God.
Charles Swindoll

When an honest soul can get still before
the living Christ, we can still hear Him say
simply and clearly, "Love the Lord your God
with all your heart and with all your soul and
with all your mind…and love one another
as I have loved you."
Gloria Gaither

The remedy for distractions is the same now
as it was in earlier and simpler times:
prayer, meditation, and the cultivation
of the inner life.
A. W. Tozer

Silence is as fit a garment for devotion
as any other language.
C.H. Spurgeon

A Tip for Today

**Find the best time of the day
to spend with God:**
Hudson Taylor, an English Missionary, wrote,
"Whatever is your best time in the day,
give that to communion with God."
That's powerful advice that leads to
a powerful faith.

A Prayer for Today

Dear Lord, in the quiet moments of this day,
I will turn my thoughts and prayers to You. In
these silent moments, I will sense Your presence,
and I will seek Your will for my life, knowing
that when I accept Your peace, I will be blessed
today and throughout eternity. Amen

No Temper Tantrums, Please

Everyone should be quick to listen, slow to speak and slow to become angry, for man's anger does not bring about the righteous life that God desires.

James 1:19, 20 NIV

*I*f you're like most guys, you know a thing or two about anger. After all, everybody gets mad occasionally, and you're probably no exception.

Anger is a natural human emotion that is sometimes necessary and appropriate. Even Jesus became angry when confronted with the moneychangers in the temple: "And Jesus entered the temple and drove out all those who were buying and selling in the temple, and overturned the tables of the moneychangers and the seats of those who were selling doves" (Matthew 21:12 NASB).

Righteous indignation is an appropriate response to evil, but God does not intend that anger should rule our lives. Far from it. God intends that we turn away from anger whenever possible and forgive our neighbors just as we seek forgiveness for ourselves.

Life is full of frustrations: some great and some small. On occasion, you, like Jesus, will confront evil, and when you do, you may respond as He did: vigorously and without reservation. But, more often your frustrations will be of the more mundane variety. As long as you live here on earth, you will face countless opportunities to lose your temper over small, relatively insignificant events: a traffic jam, an inconsiderate comment, or a broken promise. When you are tempted to lose your temper over the minor inconveniences of life, don't. Instead of turning up the heat, walk away. Turn away from anger, hatred, bitterness, and regret. Turn, instead, to God. When you do, you'll be following His commandments and giving yourself a priceless gift…the gift of peace.

Thoughts for Today

Anger breeds remorse in the heart,
discord in the home, bitterness in
the community, and confusion in the state.
Billy Graham

Anger is the noise of the soul;
the unseen irritant of the heart;
the relentless invader of silence.
Max Lucado

A Tip for Today

Count to ten . . . but don't stop there!
If you're angry with someone, don't say
the first thing that comes to your mind. Instead,
catch your breath and start counting until you
are once again in control of your temper. If you
count to a thousand and you're still counting,
go to bed! You'll feel better in the morning.

A Prayer for Today

Lord, I can be so impatient, and I can
become so angry. Calm me down, Lord, and
give me the maturity and the wisdom
to be a patient, forgiving Christian.
Just as You have forgiven me, Father,
let me forgive others so that I can
follow the example of Your Son. Amen

Failure and God's Faithfulness

If we confess our sins to him, he is faithful
and just to forgive us
and to cleanse us from every wrong.
1 John 1:9 NLT

If you've led a perfect life with absolutely no foul ups, blunders, mistakes, or flops, you can skip this chapter. But if you're like the rest of us, you know that occasional disappointments and failures are an inevitable part of life. These setbacks are simply the price of growing up and learning about life. But even when you experience bitter disappointments, you must never lose faith.

When times are tough, the Bible teaches us to persevere: "For you need endurance, so that after you have done God's will, you may receive what was promised." These reassuring words from Hebrews 10:36 (HCSB) remind us that when we persevere, we will eventually receive that which God has promised. Even when we fail, God is faithful. What's required of us is perseverance, not perfection.

When we encounter the inevitable difficulties of life here on earth, God stands ready to protect us. And, while we are waiting for God's plans to unfold, we can be comforted in the knowledge that our Creator can overcome any obstacle, even if we cannot.

Thoughts for Today

No matter how badly we have failed,
we can always get up and begin again.
Our God is the God of new beginnings.
Warren Wiersbe

Our problem isn't that we've failed.
Our problem is that we haven't failed enough.
We haven't been brought low enough to learn
what God wants us to learn.
Charles Swindoll

Never imagine that you can be a loser
by trusting in God.
C. H. Spurgeon

How beautiful it is to learn that grace
isn't fragile, and that in the family of God
we can fail and not be a failure.
Gloria Gaither

A Tip for Today

**You can count on God's faithfulness
in good times and bad.**

Max Lucado writes, "God's faithfulness has
never depended on the faithfulness of his
children. God is greater than our weakness.
In fact, I think, it is our weakness that reveals
how great God is." Enough said.

A Prayer for Today

Lord, sometimes I make mistakes and
fall short of Your commandments. When I do,
forgive me, Father. And help me learn from
my mistakes so that I can be a better
servant to You and a better example
to my friends and family. Amen

The Importance of Integrity

The man of integrity walks securely,
but he who takes crooked paths will be found out.
Proverbs 10:9 NIV

You've heard the old saying so many times that you know it by heart: "Honesty is the best policy." But it's also worth noting that honesty isn't always the *easiest* policy. Sometimes, the truth hurts, and sometimes, it's tough to be a person of integrity . . . tough, but essential.

Charles Swindoll correctly observed, "Nothing speaks louder or more powerfully than a life of integrity." Godly men agree.

Integrity is a precious thing—difficult to build but easy to tear down. As believers in Christ, we must seek to live each day with discipline, honesty, and faith. When we do, integrity becomes a habit. And God smiles.

Thoughts for Today

There's nothing like the power of integrity.
It is a characteristic so radiant, so steady, so
consistent, so beautiful, that it makes
a permanent picture in our minds.
Franklin Graham

Integrity of heart is indispensable.
John Calvin

Maintaining your integrity in a world
of sham is no small accomplishment.
Wayne Oates

Integrity is not a given factor in everyone's life.
It is a result of self-discipline, inner trust,
and a decision to be relentlessly honest
in all situations in our lives.
John Maxwell

His devotional

A Tip for Today

**One of your greatest possessions
is integrity . . . don't lose it.**
Billy Graham was right when he said:
"Integrity is the glue that holds our way
of life together. We must constantly
strive to keep our integrity intact.
When wealth is lost, nothing is lost;
when health is lost, something is lost;
when character is lost, all is lost."

A Prayer for Today

Lord, You are my Father in Heaven.
You search my heart and know me far
better than I know myself. May I be
Your worthy servant, and may I live
according to Your commandments. Let
me be a person of integrity, Lord, and
let my words and deeds be a testimony
to You, today and always. Amen

28

Your Problems... and God's Solutions

People who do what is right may have many problems,
but the Lord will solve them all.

Psalm 34:19 NCV

L ife is an adventure in problem-solving. The question is not *whether* we will encounter problems; the real question is *how* we will choose to address them. When it comes to solving the problems of everyday living, we often know precisely what needs to be done, but we may be slow in doing it—especially if what needs to be done is difficult. So we put off till tomorrow what should be done today.

As a young man living here in the 21st-century, you have your own set of challenges. As you face those challenges, you may be comforted by this fact: Trouble, of every kind, is temporary. Yet God's grace is eternal. And worries, of every kind, are temporary. But God's love is everlasting. The troubles that concern you will pass. God remains. And for every problem, God has a solution.

The words of Psalm 34 remind us that the Lord solves problems for "people who do what is right." And usually, doing "what is right" means doing the uncomfortable work of confronting our problems sooner rather than later. So with no further ado, let the problem-solving begin . . . right now.

Thoughts for Today

Let God's promises shine on your problems.
Corrie ten Boom

I choose joy. I will refuse the temptation to be
cynical; cynicism is the tool of a lazy thinker.
I will refuse to see people as anything less than
human beings, created by God. I will refuse to
see any problem as anything less than
an opportunity to see God.
Max Lucado

There is a world of difference between a person
who has a big problem and a person
who makes a problem big.
John Maxwell

The happiest people in the world are not those
who have no problems, but the people
who have learned to live with those things
that are less than perfect.
James Dobson

A Tip for Today

If It Wasn't for Trouble . . .
we might think we could handle
our lives by ourselves.

Jim Cymbala writes, "Trouble is one of
God's great servants because it reminds us
how much we continually need the Lord."
We should thank the Lord for challenges
that bring us closer to Him.

A Prayer for Today

Lord, sometimes my problems are simply
too big for me, but they are never too big
for You. Let me turn my troubles over to You,
Lord, and let me trust in You today
and for all eternity. Amen

Prayer Power

And when they had prayed, the place was shaken where they were assembled together; and they were all filled with the Holy Ghost, and they spake the word of God with boldness.

Acts 4:31 KJV

Are you a prayer warrior or have you retreated from God's battlefield? Do you pray about almost everything or about almost nothing? Do you pray only at mealtimes, or do you pray at all times? The answer to these questions will determine, to a surprising extent, the degree to which God will use you for the glory of His kingdom.

Jesus made it clear to His disciples: they should pray always. And so should we. Genuine, heartfelt prayer changes things and it changes us. When we lift our hearts to our Father in heaven, we open ourselves to a never-ending source of divine wisdom and infinite love.

Your prayers are powerful, so pray. And as you go about your daily activities, remember God's instructions: "Rejoice always! Pray constantly. Give thanks in everything, for this is God's will for you in Christ Jesus" (1 Thessalonians 5:16-18 HCSB). Start praying in the morning and keep praying until you fall off to sleep at night. And rest assured: God is always listening, and He always wants to hear from you.

Thoughts for Today

If the spiritual life is to be healthy and
under the full power of the Holy Spirit,
praying without ceasing will be natural.
Andrew Murray

Next to the wonder of seeing my Savior will be,
I think, the wonder that I made so little use
of the power of prayer.
D. L. Moody

Those who know God the best are
the richest and the most powerful in prayer.
Little acquaintance with God makes prayer
a rare and feeble thing.
E. M. Bounds

When we pray, we have linked ourselves with
Divine purposes, and we therefore have
Divine power at our disposal for human living.
E. Stanley Jones

A Tip for Today

Sometimes, the answer is "No."
God doesn't grant all of our requests,
nor should He. We must understand that
our prayers are answered by a sovereign,
all-knowing God, and that we must trust
His answers, whether the answer is
"Yes," "No," or "Not Yet."

A Prayer for Today

Dear Lord, let me raise my hopes and my
dreams, my worries and my fears to You.
Let me be a worthy example to family
and friends, showing them the importance
and the power of prayer. Let me take
everything to You in prayer, Lord,
and when I do, let me trust in
Your answers. Amen

Service with a Smile

But whosoever will be great among you, let him be your minister;
and whosoever will be chief among you, let him be your servant:
even as the Son of man came not to be ministered unto,
but to minister, and to give his life a ransom for many.
Matthew 20:26-28 KJV

T he words of Jesus are clear: The most esteemed men and women in this world are not the big-shots who jump up on stage and hog the spotlight; the greatest among us are those who are willing to become humble servants.

Are you willing to become a servant for Christ? Are you willing to pitch in and make the world a better place, or are you determined to keep all your blessings to yourself? Hopefully, you are determined to follow Christ's example by making yourself an unselfish servant to those who need your help.

Today, you may be tempted to take more than you give. But if you feel the urge to be selfish, resist that urge with all your might. Don't be stingy, selfish, or self-absorbed. Instead, serve your friends quietly and without fanfare. Find a need and fill it . . . humbly. Lend a helping hand…anonymously. Share a word of kindness . . . with quiet sincerity. As you go about your daily activities, remember that the Savior of all humanity made Himself a servant, and we, as His followers, must do no less.

Thoughts for Today

It's no secret. The ministry of the church is
a genuine concern for others. We need to stop
talking about it and start doing it. Rise and
shine friend. Everyone you meet today is
on heaven's Most Wanted list.
Charles Swindoll

It's not difficult to make an impact on your
world. All you really have to do is put the needs
of others ahead of your own. You can make
a difference with a little time and a big heart.
James Dobson

Ministry is not something we do for God;
it is something God does in and through us.
Warren Wiersbe

Jesus draws near to those who are suffering—
especially when the suffering is for His sake.
Anne Graham Lotz

A Tip for Today

Talk is cheap.
Real ministry has legs.
When it comes to serving others,
make sure that you back up your words
with deeds.

A Prayer for Today

Lord, make me a loving, encouraging,
compassionate Christian. And let my
love for Christ be reflected through
the kindness that I show to my family,
to my friends, and to all who need
the healing touch of the Master's hand.

Amen

Thanksgiving and Thanksliving

Enter his gates with thanksgiving, go into his courts
with praise. Give thanks to him and bless his name.
Psalm 100:4 NLT

Are you basically a thankful guy? Do you appreciate the stuff you've got and the life that you're privileged to live? You most certainly *should* be thankful. After all, when you stop to think about it, God has given you more blessings than you can count. So the question of the day is this: will you slow down long enough to thank your Heavenly Father . . . or not?

Sometimes, life here on earth can be complicated, demanding, and frustrating. When the demands of life leave you rushing from place to place with scarcely a moment to spare, you may fail to pause and thank your Creator for the countless blessings He has given you. Failing to thank God is understandable . . . but it's wrong.

God's Word makes it clear: A wise heart is a thankful heart. Period. Your Heavenly Father has blessed you beyond measure, and you owe Him everything, including your thanks. God is always listening—are you willing to say thanks? It's up to you, and the next move is yours.

Thoughts for Today

The devil moves in when a Christian starts
to complain, but thanksgiving in the Spirit
defeats the devil and glorifies the Lord.
Warren Wiersbe

The heathen misrepresent God by worshipping
idols; we misrepresent God by our murmuring
and our complaining.
C. H. Spurgeon

Why wait until the fourth Thursday
in November? Thanksgiving to
God should be an everyday affair.
The time to be thankful is now!
Jim Gallery

It is always possible to be thankful for
what is given rather than to complain about
what is not given. One or the other becomes
a habit of life.
Elisabeth Elliot

A Tip for Today

**When Is the Best Time to Say
"Thanks" to God?**
Any time. God loves you all the time,
and that's exactly why you should
praise Him all the time.

A Prayer for Today

Dear Lord, sometimes, amid the demands
of the day, I lose perspective, and
I fail to give thanks for Your
blessings and for Your love. Today,
help me to count those blessings,
and let me give thanks to You, Father,
for Your love, for Your grace,
for Your blessings,
and for Your Son. Amen

Christ's Love

Do you think anyone is going to be able to drive a wedge between us and Christ's love for us? There is no way! Not trouble, not hard times, not hatred, not hunger, not homelessness, not bullying threats, not backstabbing, not even the worst sins listed in Scripture...I'm absolutely convinced that nothing, nothing living or dead, angelic or demonic, today or tomorrow, high or low, thinkable or unthinkable, absolutely nothing can get between us and God's love because of the way that Jesus our Master has embraced us.

Romans 8:35,38, 39 MSG

How much does Christ love us? More than we, as mere mortals, can comprehend. His love is perfect and steadfast. Even though we are fallible and wayward, the Good Shepherd cares for us still. Even though we have fallen far short of the Father's commandments, Christ loves us with a power and depth that is beyond our understanding. The sacrifice that Jesus made upon the cross was made for each of us, and His love endures to the edge of eternity and beyond.

Christ's love changes everything. When you accept His gift of grace, you are transformed, not only for today, but also for all eternity. If you haven't already done so, accept Jesus Christ as Your Savior. He's waiting patiently for you to invite Him into your heart. Please don't make Him wait a single minute longer.

Thoughts for Today

He loved us not because we're lovable,
but because He is love.
C. S. Lewis

So Jesus came, stripping himself of everything
as he came—omnipotence, omniscience,
omnipresence—everything except love.
"He emptied himself" (Philippians 2:7),
emptied himself of everything except love.
Love—his only protection, his only weapon,
his only method.
E. Stanley Jones

If you come to Christ, you will always have
the option of an ever-present friend.
You don't have to dial long-distance.
He'll be with you every step of the way.
Bill Hybels

A Tip for Today

Jesus Loves Me, This I Know . . .
But How Much?

Here's how much: Jesus loves you so much that He gave His life so that you might live forever with Him in heaven. And how can you repay Christ's love? By accepting Him into your heart and by obeying His rules. When you do, He will love you and bless you today, tomorrow, and forever.

A Prayer for Today

Dear Lord, I offer thanksgiving and praise for the gift of Your only begotten Son. His love is boundless, infinite, and eternal. And, as an expression of my love for Him, let me share His message with my family, with my friends, and with the world. Amen

It's
a New Day

The inward man is being renewed day by day.
2 Corinthians 4:16 NKJV

Even the most inspired Christian guys can find themselves running on empty. Even the most well-intentioned guys can run out of energy; even the most hopeful believers can be burdened by fears and doubts. And you are no exception.

When you're exhausted, or worried—or worse—there is a source from which you can draw the power needed to recharge your spiritual batteries. That source is God.

God intends that His children lead joyous lives filled with abundance and peace. But sometimes, abundance and peace seem very far away. During these difficult days, we must turn to God for renewal, and when we do, He will restore us.

Are you tired or troubled? Turn your heart toward God in prayer. Are you weak or worried? Take the time—or, more accurately, *make* the time—to delve deeply into God's Holy Word. Are you spiritually depleted? Call upon fellow believers to support you, and call upon Christ to renew your spirit and your life. When you do, you'll discover that the Creator of the universe stands always ready and always able to create a new sense of wonderment and joy *in you*.

Thoughts for Today

Like a spring of pure water, God's peace
in our hearts brings cleansing and
refreshment to our minds and bodies.
Billy Graham

Our Father will refresh us with many pleasant
inns on the journey, but he would not
encourage us to mistake them for home.
C. S. Lewis

I wish I could make it all new again; I can't.
But God can. "He restores my soul," wrote
the shepherd. God doesn't reform; he restores.
He doesn't camouflage the old; he restores
the new. The Master Builder will pull out the
original plan and restore it. He will restore
the vigor, he will restore the energy. He will
restore the hope. He will restore the soul.
Max Lucado

A Tip for Today

Big, Bigger, and Very Big Plans.
God has very big plans in store for your life,
so trust Him and wait patiently for those
plans to unfold. And remember:
God's timing is best.

A Prayer for Today

Heavenly Father, sometimes I am
troubled, and sometimes I grow weary.
When I am weak, Lord, give me strength.
When I am discouraged, renew me.
When I am fearful, let me feel Your
healing touch. Let me always trust in
Your promises, Lord, and let me draw
strength from those promises and
from Your unending love. Amen

11

Be Quick to Forgive

Be gentle with one another, sensitive. Forgive one another
as quickly and thoroughly as God in Christ forgave you.
Ephesians 4:32 MSG

Are you the kind of guy who carries a grudge? If so, you know sometimes it's very tough to forgive the people who have hurt you. And that's too bad because life would be much simpler if we could forgive people "once and for all" and be done with it. But forgiveness is seldom that easy. For most of us, the decision to forgive is straightforward, but the process of forgiving is more difficult. Forgiveness is a journey that requires effort, time, perseverance, and prayer.

Forgiveness is seldom easy, but it is always right. When we forgive those who have hurt us, we honor God by obeying His commandments. But when we harbor bitterness against others, we disobey God—with predictably unhappy results.

If there exists even one person whom you have not forgiven (and that includes yourself), follow God's commandment and His will for your life: forgive that person today. And remember that bitterness, anger, and regret are not part of God's plan for your life. Forgiveness is.

If you sincerely wish to forgive someone, pray for that person. And then pray for yourself by asking God to heal your heart. Don't expect forgiveness to be easy or quick, but rest assured: with God as your partner, you *can* forgive . . . and *you will*.

Thoughts for Today

Every time we forgive others, deserving it or not, we have a reminder of God's forgiveness.
Franklin Graham

Looking back over my life, all I can see is mercy and grace written in large letters everywhere. May God help me have the same kind of heart toward those who wound or offend me.
Jim Cymbala

An eye for an eye and a tooth for a tooth . . . and pretty soon, everybody's blind and wearing dentures.
Anonymous

his devotional

A Tip for Today

Holding a grudge?
Drop it.
Never expect other people to be
more forgiving than you are.
And remember:
the best time to forgive is now.

A Prayer for Today

Dear Lord, when I am bitter,
You can change my unforgiving heart.
And, when I am slow to forgive,
Your Word reminds me that forgiveness
is Your commandment. Let me be
Your obedient servant, Lord, and let me
forgive others just as You have
forgiven me. Amen

All the Strength You Need

I am able to do all things through Him who strengthens me.
Philippians 4:13 HCSB

here do you go to find strength? The gym? The health food store? The espresso bar? There's a better source of strength, of course, and that source is God. He is a never-ending source of strength and courage *if* you call upon Him.

Are you an energized Christian? You should be. But if you're not, you must seek strength and renewal from the source that will never fail: that source, of course, is your Heavenly Father. And rest assured—when you sincerely petition Him, He will give you all the strength you need to live victoriously for Him.

Have you "tapped in" to the power of God? Have you turned your life and your heart over to Him, or are you muddling along under your own power? The answer to this question will determine the quality of your life here on earth and the destiny of your life throughout all eternity. So start tapping in—and remember that when it comes to strength, God is the Ultimate Source.

Thoughts for Today

God is great and God is powerful, but
we must invite him to be powerful in our lives.
His strength is always there, but it's up to us to
provide a channel through which
that power can flow.
Bill Hybels

Prayer plumes the wings of God's young eaglets
so that they may learn to mount above
the clouds. Prayer brings inner strength to
God's warriors and sends them forth to
spiritual battle with their muscles firm
and their armor in place.
C. H. Spurgeon

God is the One who provides our strength,
not only to cope with the demands of the day,
but also to rise above them. May we look to
Him for the strength to soar.
Jim Gallery

A Tip for Today

Need Strength?
Let God's Spirit Reign Over Your Heart.
Anne Graham Lotz writes, "The amount of
power you experience to live a victorious,
triumphant Christian life is directly
proportional to the freedom you give
the Spirit to be Lord of your life!"
And remember that the best time to begin
living triumphantly is the present moment.

A Prayer for Today

Dear Lord, I will turn to You for strength.
When my responsibilities seem
overwhelming, I will trust You to give
me courage and perspective. Today
and every day, I will look to You as
the ultimate source of my hope, my strength,
my peace, and my salvation. Amen

Discovering Your Talents

God has given gifts to each of you from his great variety
of spiritual gifts. Manage them well so that
God's generosity can flow through you.

1 Peter 4:10 NLT

W hen God made you, he equipped you with an array of talents and abilities that are uniquely yours. It's up to you to discover those talents and to use them, but sometimes the world will encourage you to do otherwise. At times, our society will attempt to cubbyhole you, to standardize you, and to make you fit into a particular, preformed mold. Perhaps God has other plans.

Have you found something in this life that you're passionate about? Something that inspires you to jump out of bed in the morning and hit the ground running? And does your work honor the Creator by making His world a better place? If so, congratulations: you're using your gifts well.

Sometimes, because you're an imperfect human being, you may become so wrapped up in meeting *society's* expectations that you fail to focus on *God's* expectations. To do so is a mistake of major proportions—don't make it. Instead, seek God's guidance as you focus your energies on becoming the best "you" that you can possibly be.

What's the best way to thank God for the gifts that He has given you? By using them. And you might as well start using those gifts today.

Thoughts for Today

Find satisfaction in him who made you,
and only then find satisfaction in yourself
as part of his creation.
St. Augustine

You are valuable just because you exist.
Not because of what you do or what
you have done, but simply because you are.
Max Lucado

A healthy self-identity is seeing yourself as
God sees you—no more and no less.
Josh McDowell

A Tip for Today

Converting Talent Into Skill Requires Work:
Remember the old adage:
"What we are is God's gift to us; what we
become is our gift to God."

A Prayer for Today

Lord, I have so much to
learn and so many ways to
improve myself, but You love
me just as I am. Thank You
for Your love and for Your
Son. And help me to become
the person that You want me
to become. Amen

Times That Test Your Faith

The fundamental fact of existence is that this trust in God,
this faith, is the firm foundation under everything
that makes life worth living.

Hebrews 11:1 MSG

I n the months and years ahead, your faith will be tested many times. Every life—including yours—is a series of successes and failures, celebrations and disappointments, joys and sorrows. Every step of the way, through every triumph and tragedy, God will stand by your side and strengthen you…if you have faith in Him. Jesus taught His disciples that if they had faith, they could move mountains. You can too.

If you place your faith, your trust, indeed your life in the hands of Christ Jesus, you'll be amazed at the marvelous things He can do with you and through you.

Today and every day, strengthen your faith through praise, through worship, through Bible study, and through prayer. God has big plans for you, so trust His plans and strengthen your faith in Him. With God, all things are possible, and He stands ready to help you accomplish miraculous things with your life…*if* you have faith.

Thoughts for Today

Hope is nothing more than the expectation
of those things which faith has believed to be
truly promised by God.
John Calvin

Faith is a living, daring confidence in God's
grace, so sure and certain that a man would
stake his life on it a thousand times.
Martin Luther

Faith never knows where it is being led or it
would not be faith. True faith is content to
travel under sealed orders.
Oswald Chambers

Faith means believing in advance what will
only make sense in reverse.
Philip Yancey

A Tip for Today

**Faith Should Be Practiced
More Than Studied.**

Vance Havner said, "Nothing is more
disastrous than to study faith, analyze faith,
make noble resolves of faith, but
never actually to make *the leap* of faith."
How true!

A Prayer for Today

Dear Lord, direct my path far from
the temptations and distractions of
this world, and make me a champion of
the faith. Today I will honor You with
my thoughts, my actions, and my prayers.
I will worship You, Father, with thanksgiving
in my heart and praise on my lips,
this day and forever. Amen

15

Hang in There

Let us run with endurance the race that is set before us, looking unto Jesus, the author and finisher of our faith, who for the joy that was set before Him endured the cross, despising the shame, and has sat down at the right hand of the throne of God.

Hebrews 12:1, 2 NKJV

A well-lived life is like a marathon, not a sprint—it calls for preparation, determination, and *lots* of perseverance. As an example of perfect perseverance, we Christians need look no further than our Savior, Jesus Christ.

Jesus finished what He began. Despite His suffering, despite the shame of the cross, Jesus was steadfast in His faithfulness to God. We, too, must remain faithful, especially during times of hardship. Sometimes, God may answer our prayers with silence, and when He does, we must patiently persevere.

Are you facing a difficult time in your life? If so, remember the words of Winston Churchill: "Never give in!" And remember this: whatever your problem, God can handle it. Your job is to keep persevering until He does.

Thoughts for Today

Battles are won in the trenches, in the grit
and grime of courageous determination;
they are won day by day in the arena of life.
Charles Swindoll

That is the source of Jeremiah's living
persistence, his creative constancy.
He was up before the sun, listening to
God's word. Rising early, he was quiet
and attentive before his Lord. Long before
the yelling started, the mocking,
the complaining, there was this centering,
discovering, exploring time with God.
Eugene Peterson

Don't give up. Moses was once a basket case!
Anonymous

A Tip for Today

The World Encourages Instant Gratification but God's Work Takes Time.
Remember the words of C. H. Spurgeon:
"By perseverance, the snail reached the ark."

A Prayer for Today

Dear Lord, life is not a sprint, but a marathon. When the pace of my life becomes frantic, slow me down and give me perspective. Keep me steady and sure. When I become weary, let me persevere so that, in Your time, I might finish my work here on earth, and that You might then say, "Well done my good and faithful servant." Amen

16

Nothing to Fear

Be strong and courageous.
Do not be terrified; do not be discouraged,
for the Lord your God will be with you wherever you go.
Joshua 1:9 NIV

Every human life (including yours) is a tapestry of events: some grand, some not-so-grand, and some downright disheartening. When we reach the mountaintops of life, praising God is easy. But, when the storm clouds form overhead and we find ourselves in the dark valley of despair, our faith is stretched, sometimes to the breaking point. As Christians, we can be comforted: Wherever we find ourselves, whether at the top of the mountain or the depths of the valley, God is there, and because He cares for us, we can live courageously.

Believing Christians have every reason to be courageous. After all, the ultimate battle has already been fought and won on the cross at Calvary. But, even dedicated followers of Christ may find their courage tested by the inevitable disappointments and tragedies that occur in the lives of believers and non-believers alike.

The next time you find your courage tested to the limit, remember that God is as near as your next breath, and remember that He offers salvation to His children. He is your shield and your strength; He is your protector and your deliverer. Call upon Him in your hour of need and then be comforted. Whatever your challenge, whatever your trouble, God can handle it. And will.

Thoughts for Today

Courage is contagious.
Billy Graham

Take courage. We walk in the wilderness today and in the Promised Land tomorrow.
D. L. Moody

Faith is stronger than fear.
John Maxwell

A Tip for Today

Jesus Is Looking for a Few Good Men . . .
Like You.

Charles Swindoll writes,
"Our Lord is searching for people who will
make a difference. Christians dare not dissolve
into the background or blend into
the neutral scenery of the world."

A Prayer for Today

Lord, sometimes I face challenges that leave me
breathless. When I am fearful, let me lean upon
You. Keep me ever mindful, Lord, that You are
my God, my strength, and my shield. With You
by my side, I have nothing to fear. And,
with Your Son, Jesus as my Savior, I have received
the priceless gift of eternal life. Help me
to be a grateful and courageous servant
this day and every day. Amen

Today
Is a Gift . . .
Use It

While it is daytime, we must continue doing the work
of the One who sent me.
Night is coming, when no one can work.

John 9:4 NCV

he words of John 9:4 remind us that "night is coming" for all of us. But until then, God gives us each day and fills it to the brim with possibilities. The day is presented to us fresh and clean at midnight, free of charge, but we must beware: Today is a non-renewable resource—once it's gone, it's gone forever. Our responsibility, of course, is to use this day in the service of God's will and in accordance with His commandments.

Today is a priceless gift that has been given to you by God—don't waste it. Don't stand on the sidelines as life's parade passes you by. Instead, search for the hidden possibilities that God has placed along your path. This day is a one-of-a-kind treasure that can be put to good use—or not. Your challenge is to use this day joyfully and productively. And while you're at it, encourage others to do likewise. After all, night is coming when no one can work . . .

Thoughts for Today

When we truly walk with God throughout
our day, life slowly starts to fall into place.
Bill Hybels

With each new dawn, life delivers a package to
your front door, rings your doorbell, and runs.
Charles Swindoll

Today is mine. Tomorrow is none of my
business. If I peer anxiously into the fog of
the future, I will strain my spiritual eyes
so that I will not see clearly
what is required of me now.
Elisabeth Elliot

Wherever you are, be all there.
Live to the hilt every situation
you believe to be the will of God.
Jim Elliot

Today Is a Gift...Use It

his devotional

A Tip for Today

**Remember the beautiful words found in
the 118th Psalm:**
"This is the day which the LORD has made;
let us rejoice and be glad in it" (v. 24).
The present moment is a priceless gift.
Treasure it; savor it; and use it.

A Prayer for Today

Help me, Father, to learn from the past but not
live in it. And, help me to plan for the future
but not to worry about it. This is the day that
You have given me, Lord. Let me use it according
to Your master plan, and let me give thanks for
Your blessings. Enable me to live each moment to
the fullest, totally involved in Your will. Amen

Living on Purpose

God chose you to be his people,
so I urge you now to live the life to which God called you.
Ephesians 4:1 NCV

"**W**hat did God put me here to do?" If you're like most guys, you've asked yourself that question on many occasions. Perhaps you have pondered over your future, uncertain of your plans, unsure of your next step. But even if you don't have a clear plan for the next step of your life's journey, you may rest assured that God does.

God has a plan for the universe, and He has a plan for you. He understands that plan as thoroughly and completely as He knows you. If you seek God's will earnestly and prayerfully, He will make His plans known to you in His own time and in His own way.

Do you sincerely seek to discover God's purpose for your life? If so, you must first be willing to live in accordance with His commandments. You must also study God's Word and be watchful for His signs. Finally, you should open yourself up to the Creator every day—beginning with this one—and you must have faith that He will soon reveal His plans to you.

Sometimes, God's plans and purposes may seem unmistakably clear to you. If so, push ahead. But other times, He may lead you through the wilderness before He directs you to the Promised Land. So be patient and keep seeking His will for your life. When you do, you'll be amazed at the marvelous things that an all-powerful, all-knowing God can do.

Thoughts for Today

Nothing in this world is without meaning.
A. W. Tozer

It's incredible to realize
that what we do each day has meaning
in the big picture of God's plan.
Bill Hybels

A Tip for Today

**Discovering God's Purpose for Your Life
Is Continuing Education.**

God's plan is unfolding day by day. If you
keep your eyes and your heart open,
He'll reveal His plans. God has big things in
store for you, but He may have quite a few
lessons to teach you *before* you
are fully prepared to do His will and
fulfill His purposes.

A Prayer for Today

Dear Lord, I seek to live a meaningful life;
I will turn to You to find that meaning. I will study
Your Word, I will obey Your commandments,
I will trust Your providence, and I will honor
Your Son. Give me Your blessings, Father, and
lead me along a path that is pleasing to You,
today, tomorrow, and forever. Amen

Praising
the Lord

From the rising of the sun to its setting,
the name of the LORD is to be praised.
Psalm 113:3 NASB

hen is the best time to praise God? In church? Before dinner is served? When we tuck little children into bed? None of the above. The best time to praise God is all day, every day, to the greatest extent we can, with thanksgiving in our hearts, and with a song on our lips.

Too many of us, even well-intentioned believers, tend to "compartmentalize" our waking hours into a few familiar categories: work, rest, play, family time, and worship. To do so is a mistake. Worship and praise should be woven into the fabric of everything we do; it should never be relegated to a weekly three-hour visit to church on Sunday morning.

Theologian Wayne Oates once admitted, "Many of my prayers are made with my eyes open. You see, it seems I'm always praying about something, and it's not always convenient—or safe—to close my eyes." Dr. Oates understood that God always hears our prayers and that the relative position of our eyelids is of no concern to Him.

Today, find a little more time to lift your concerns to God in prayer, and praise Him for all that He has done. Whether your eyes are open or closed, He's listening.

Thoughts for Today

Be not afraid of saying too much in
the praises of God; all the danger
is of saying too little.
Matthew Henry

Praise—lifting up our heart and hands,
exulting with our voices, singing his praises—
is the occupation of those
who dwell in the kingdom.
Max Lucado

A Tip for Today

Praise Him!

One of the main reasons you go to church is to praise God. But, you need not wait until Sunday rolls around to thank your Heavenly Father. Instead, you can praise Him many times each day by saying silent prayers that only He can hear.

A Prayer for Today

Dear Lord, I will praise You today and every day that I live. And, I will praise Your Son, the Savior of my life. Christ's love is boundless and eternal. Let my thoughts, my prayers, my words, and my deeds praise Him now and forever. Amen

God Said It... and That Settles It

Let us hold on to the confession of our hope without wavering, for He who promised is faithful.

Hebrews 10:23 HCSB

Christianity is based upon promises that are contained in a unique book. That book is the Holy Bible. The Bible is a roadmap for life here on earth and for life eternal. As Christians, we are called upon to study its meaning, to trust its promises, to follow its commandments, and to share its Good News.

As believers, we should study the Bible each day and meditate upon its meaning for our lives. Otherwise, we deprive ourselves of a priceless gift from our Creator. God's Holy Word is, indeed, a transforming, life-changing, one-of-a-kind treasure. And, a passing acquaintance with the Good Book is insufficient for Christians who seek to obey God's Word and understand His will.

God has made promises to you, and He intends to keep them. So take God at His word: trust His promises and share them with your family, with your friends, and with the world.

Thoughts for Today

Only God knows when everything in and around is fully ripe for the manifestation of the blessings that have been given to faith (Mark 11:24). It is through faith and patience we inherit the promises.
Andrew Murray

We honor God by asking for great things when they are a part of His promise. We dishonor Him and cheat ourselves when we ask for molehills where He has promised mountains.
Vance Hayner

We must depend upon the performance of the promise when all the doors leading up to it are shut.
Matthew Henry

A Tip for Today

Trust God's Word:

Charles Swindoll writes,
" There are four words I wish we would never
forget, and they are, 'God keeps his word.'"
And remember: When it comes to *studying*
God's Word, school is always in session.

A Prayer for Today

Dear God, the Bible contains many
promises. Let me trust Your promises,
and let me live according to
Your Holy Word, not just for today,
but forever. Amen

Do as I Say... and as I Do

In every way be an example of doing good deeds.
When you teach, do it with honesty and seriousness.

Titus 2:7 NCV

Like it or not, all of us are examples. The question is not whether we will be examples to our families and friends; the question is simply what kind of examples will we be.

What kind of example are you? Are you the kind of person whose life serves as a powerful example of righteousness? Are you a young man whose behavior serves as a positive role model for younger folks? Are you the kind of guy whose actions, day in and day out, are honorable, ethical, and admirable? If so, you are not only blessed by God, you are also a powerful force for good in a world that desperately needs positive influences such as yours.

D. L. Moody advised, "A man ought to live so that everybody knows he is a Christian, and most of all, his family ought to know." And that's sound advice because our families and friends are watching . . . and so, for that matter, is God.

Thoughts for Today

Men are mirrors, or "carriers" of Christ
to other men. Sometimes unconscious carriers.
C. S. Lewis

More depends on my walk than my talk.
D. L. Moody

We urgently need people who encourage and
inspire us to move toward God and away from
the world's enticing pleasures.
Jim Cymbala

There is too much sermonizing and
too little witnessing. People do not come to
Christ at the end of an argument.
Vance Havner

A Tip for Today

Living Your Life and Shining Your Light . . .
As a Christian, the most important light
you shine is the light that your own life
shines on the lives of others. May your light
shine brightly, righteously, obediently,
and eternally!

A Prayer for Today

Lord, make me a worthy example to
my family and friends. And, let my words
and my actions show people how my life
has been changed by You. I will praise
You, Father, by following in the footsteps
of Your Son. Let others see Him
through me. Amen

Kindness
Is a Choice

Kind people do themselves a favor,
but cruel people bring trouble on themselves.
Proverbs 11:17 NCV

*I*f we believe the words of Proverbs 11:17
—and we should—then we understand
that kindness is its own reward. And, if we
obey the commandments of our Savior—and
we should—we must sow seeds of kindness
wherever we go.

Kindness is a choice. Sometimes, when
we feel happy or generous, we find it easy
to be kind. Other times, when we are
discouraged or tired, we can scarcely summon
the energy to utter a single kind word. But,
God's commandment is clear: He intends
that we make the conscious choice to treat
others with kindness and respect, no matter
our circumstances, no matter our emotions.
Kindness, therefore, is a choice that we, as
Christians, must make many times each day.

Kindness, compassion, and forgiveness
are hallmarks of your Christian faith. So
today, in honor of the One who first showed
compassion for you, it's *your* turn to teach your
family and friends the art of kindness through
your words and deeds. And then, you can open
your arms wide to receive the gifts that God
has in store for believers (like you) who are
willing to obey His Holy Word.

Thoughts for Today

When you extend hospitality to others,
you're not trying to impress people,
you're trying to reflect God to them.
Max Lucado

Do all the good you can. By all the means
you can. In all the ways you can. In all the
places you can. At all the times you can. To all
the people you can. As long as ever you can.
John Wesley

The mark of a Christian is that he will walk
the second mile and turn the other cheek.
A wise man or woman gives the extra effort,
all for the glory of the Lord Jesus Christ.
John Maxwell

All kindness and good deeds, we must keep
silent. The result will be an inner reservoir
of personality power.
Catherine Marshall

A Tip for Today

Kindness Every Day:
Kindness should be part of our lives every day,
not just on the days when we feel good.
Don't try to be kind some of the time, and
don't try to be kind to some of the people you
know. Instead, try to be kind all of the time,
and try to be kind to all the people you know.
Remember, the Golden Rule starts with you!

A Prayer for Today

Lord, make me a loving, encouraging
Christian. And, let my love for Christ
be reflected through the kindness that
I show to those who need the healing
touch of the Master's hand. Amen

Grace for Living

For if, by the trespass of the one man, death reigned through that one man, how much more will those who receive God's abundant provision of grace and of the gift of righteousness reign in life through the one man, Jesus Christ.

Romans 5:17 NIV

ere's the great news: God's grace is not earned . . . and thank goodness it's not! If God's grace were some sort of reward for good behavior, none of us could earn enough Brownie Points to win the big prize. But it doesn't work that way. Grace is a free offer from God. By accepting that offer, we transform our lives today and forever.

God's grace is not just any old gift; it's *the ultimate gift*, and we owe Him our eternal gratitude. Our Heavenly Father is waiting patiently for each of us to accept His Son and receive His grace. Let us accept that gift today so that we might enjoy God's presence now *and* throughout all eternity.

God's grace is indeed a gift from the heart—God's heart. And as believers, we must accept God's precious gift thankfully, humbly, and immediately—today is never too soon because tomorrow may indeed be too late.

Thoughts for Today

The will of God will never lead you where
the grace of God cannot keep you.
Warren Wiersbe

"Grace" contains the essence of the gospel
as a drop of water can contain
the image of the sun.
Philip Yancey

The cross was heavy, the blood was real,
and the price was extravagant. It would have
bankrupted you or me, so he paid it for us.
Call it simple. Call it a gift. But don't call it
easy. Call it what it is. Call it grace.
Max Lucado

Christ is no Moses, no exactor, no giver
of laws, but a giver of grace, a Savior;
he is infinite mercy and goodness, freely and
bountifully given to us.
Martin Luther

A Tip for Today

God's Grace Is Always Available:
Jim Cymbala writes,
"No one is beyond his grace. No situation,
anywhere on earth, is too hard for God."
If you sincerely seek God's grace,
He will give it freely. So ask, and
you *will* receive.

A Prayer for Today

Lord, Your grace is a gift that cannot be earned. It is a gift that was given freely when I accepted Your Son as my personal Savior. Freely have I received Your gifts, Father. Let me freely share my gifts, my possessions, my time, my energy, and my faith. And let my words, my thoughts, my prayers, and my deeds bring honor to You and to Your Son, now and forever. Amen

24

Patience, Please!

Better a patient man than a warrior,
a man who controls his temper than one who takes a city.
Proverbs 16:32 NIV

Are you a perfectly patient fellow? If so, feel free to skip the rest of this page. But if you're not, here's something to think about: If you *really* want to become a more patient person, God is ready *and* willing to help.

The Bible promises that when you sincerely seek God's help, He will give you the things that you need—and that includes patience. But God won't *force* you to become a more patient person. If you want to become a more mature Christian, you've got to do some of the work yourself—and the best time to start doing that work is now.

So, if you want to gain patience and maturity, bow your head and start praying about it. Then, rest assured that with God's help, you can most certainly make yourself a more patient, understanding, and mature Christian.

Thoughts for Today

God never hurries. There are no deadlines
against which He must work. To know this is
to quiet our spirits and relax our nerves.
A. W. Tozer

As we wait on God, He helps us use the winds
of adversity to soar above our problems.
As the Bible says, "Those who wait on
the LORD…shall mount up with
wings like eagles."
Billy Graham

Waiting means going about our assigned tasks,
confident that God will provide
the meaning and the conclusions.
Eugene Peterson

Patience is a virtue that carries a lot of wait.
Anonymous

Patience, Please!

A Tip for Today

**Waiting Faithfully for God's Plan
To Unfold Is More Important
Than Understanding God's Plan.**
Ruth Bell Graham once said,
"When I am dealing with an all-powerful,
all-knowing God, I, as a mere mortal, must
offer my petitions not only with persistence,
but also with patience. Someday I'll know
why." Even when you can't understand
God's plans, you must trust Him
and never lose faith!

A Prayer for Today

*Heavenly Father, let me wait quietly for You.
Let me live according to Your plan and according
to Your timetable. When I am hurried, slow me
down. When I become impatient with others,
give me empathy. Today, I want to be a patient
Christian, Lord, as I trust in You and
in Your master plan. Amen*

Your Particular Gifts

Each man has his own gift from God;
one has this gift, another has that.
1 Corinthians 7:7 NIV

Face it: you've got an array of talents that need to be refined. All people possess special gifts—bestowed from the Father above—and you are no exception. But, your particular gift is no guarantee of success; it must be cultivated—by you—or it will go unused . . . and God's gift to you will be squandered.

Are you willing to do the hard work that's required to discover your talents and to develop them? If you are wise, you'll answer "yes." After all, if you don't make the most of your talents, who has the most to lose? You do!

So make a promise to yourself that you will earnestly seek to discover the talents that God has given you. Then, nourish those talents and make them grow. Finally, vow to share your gifts with the world for as long as God gives you the power to do so. After all, the best way to say "Thank You" for God's gifts is to use them.

Thoughts for Today

God is still in the process of dispensing gifts,
and He uses ordinary individuals like us
to develop those gifts in other people.
Howard Hendricks

One thing taught large in the Holy Scriptures
is that while God gives His gifts freely, He will
require a strict accounting of them at the end
of the road. Each man is personally responsible
for his store, be it large or small, and will be
required to explain his use of it before
the judgment seat of Christ.
A. W. Tozer

You are the only person on earth
who can use your ability.
Zig Ziglar

A Tip for Today

One Career or Many?

Only a generation ago, men and women
entered the workplace with the expectation
that one career might last a lifetime. For most
of us, those days are gone, probably forever.
So keep learning, and keep your eyes open
for the next big thing . . .
it's probably just around the corner.

A Prayer for Today

Lord, I praise You for Your
priceless gifts. I give thanks
for Your creation, for Your Son,
and for the unique talents and
opportunities that You have
given me. Let me use my gifts for
the glory of Your kingdom,
this day and every day. Amen

The Love of Money

For the love of money is a root of all sorts of evil,
and some by longing for it have wandered away from the faith and
pierced themselves with many griefs.

1 Timothy 6:10 NASB

Are you a guy who's overly concerned with the stuff that money can buy? Hopefully not. On the grand stage of a well-lived life, material possessions should play a rather small role. Of course, we all need the basic necessities of life, but once we meet those needs for ourselves and for our families, the piling up of possessions creates more problems than it solves. Our real riches, of course, are not of this world. We are never really rich until we are rich in spirit.

Our society is in love with money and the things that money can buy. God is not. God cares about people, not possessions, and so must we. We must, to the best of our abilities, love our neighbors as ourselves, and we must, to the best of our abilities, resist the mighty temptation to place possessions ahead of people.

Money, in and of itself, is not evil; worshiping money is. So today, as you prioritize matters of importance in your life, remember that God is almighty, but the dollar is not.

Thoughts for Today

If a person gets his attitude toward money
right, it will help straighten out almost
every other area of his life.
Billy Graham

One of the dangers of having a lot of money is
that you may be quite satisfied with the kinds
of happiness money can give and so fail to
realize your need for God. If everything seems
to come simply by signing checks, you may
forget that you are at every moment totally
dependent on God.
C. S. Lewis

God is entitled to a portion of our income.
Not because he needs it, but because
we need to give it.
James Dobson

A Tip for Today

Stuff 101:
The world says, "Buy more stuff."
God says, "Stuff isn't important."
Believe God.

A Prayer for Today

Dear Lord, help make me a responsible
steward of my financial resources.
Let me trust Your Holy Word, and
let me use my tithe for the support of
Your church and for the eternal glory of
Your Son. Amen

Perfectionism 101

Those who wait for perfect weather will never plant seeds;
those who look at every cloud will never harvest crops.
Plant early in the morning, and work until evening, because you
don't know if this or that will succeed. They might both do well.

Ecclesiastes 11:4,6 NCV

So many expectations . . . so little time!

As a guy living here in the 21st Century, you know that expectations can be very high indeed. The media delivers an endless stream of messages that tell you how to look, how to behave, how to dress, and what to drive. The media's expectations are *impossible* to meet—God's are not. God doesn't expect perfection . . . and neither should you.

If you find yourself bound up by the chains of perfectionism, it's time to ask yourself who you're trying to impress, and why. If you're trying to impress other people, it's time to reconsider your priorities. Your first responsibility is to the Heavenly Father who created you and to His Son who saved you. Then, you bear a powerful responsibility to your family. But, when it comes to meeting society's unrealistic expectations, forget it!

Remember that when you accepted Christ as your Savior, God accepted you for all eternity. Now, it's your turn to accept yourself *and* your loved ones. When you do, you'll feel a tremendous weight being lifted from your shoulders. After all, pleasing God is simply a matter of obeying His commandments and accepting His Son. But as for pleasing everybody else? That's impossible!

Thoughts for Today

The greatest destroyer of good works is
the desire to do great works.
C. H. Spurgeon

God is so inconceivably good.
He's not looking for perfection.
He already saw it in Christ.
He's looking for affection.
Beth Moore

What makes a Christian a Christian is
not perfection but forgiveness.
Max Lucado

A Tip for Today

**In This World, Strive for Excellence,
Not Perfection.**
There will be plenty of time for perfection
in the world to come.

A Prayer for Today

Dear Lord, You have taught us that
love covers a multitude of shortcomings.
Keep us mindful that perfection will be ours
in the next world, not in this one.
Help us to be accepting of our own
imperfections, and give us the wisdom
to accept—and even to cherish—
the imperfections of those we love. Amen

Temptations, Temptations, Temptations

Let us throw off everything that hinders and
the sin that so easily entangles, and let us run with perseverance
the race marked out for us.
Hebrews 12:1 NIV

H ow hard is it to bump into temptation in this crazy world? Not very hard. The devil, it seems, is out on the street, working 24/7, causing pain and heartache in more ways than ever before. We, as Christians, must remain vigilant. Not only must we resist Satan when he confronts us, but we must also avoid those places where Satan can most easily tempt us. And, if we are to avoid the unending temptations of this world, we must arm ourselves with the Word of God.

In a letter to believers, Peter offers a stern warning: "Your adversary, the devil, prowls around like a roaring lion, seeking someone to devour" (1 Peter 5:8 NASB). What was true in New Testament times is equally true in our own. Satan tempts his prey and then devours them (and it's up to you to make sure that you're *not* one of the ones being devoured!)

As believing Christians, we must beware because temptations are everywhere. Satan is determined to win; we must be equally determined that he does not.

Thoughts for Today

Abide in Jesus, the sinless one—which means,
give up all of self and its life, and dwell
in God's will and rest in His strength.
This is what brings the power
that does not commit sin.
Andrew Murray

Of two evils, choose neither.
C. H. Spurgeon

Take a really honest look at yourself.
Have any old sins begun to take control again?
This would be a wonderful time to allow Him
to bring fresh order out of longstanding chaos.
Charles Swindoll

An exalted view of God brings a clear view
of sin and a realistic view of self.
Henry Blackaby

A Tip for Today

We Live in a Temptation Generation:
You can find temptation in lots of places.
Your job is to *avoid* those places!

A Prayer for Today

Dear Lord, I am an imperfect
human being. When I have
sinned, let me repent from
my wrongdoings, and let me seek
forgiveness—first from You,
then from others,
and finally from myself. Amen

Grow Up!

Grow in grace and understanding of our Master and Savior, Jesus Christ. Glory to the Master, now and forever! Yes!

2 Peter 3:18 MSG

Are you about as mature as you're ever going to be? Hopefully not! When it comes to your faith, God doesn't intend for you to become "fully grown," at least not in this lifetime.

As a Christian man, you should continue to grow in the love and the knowledge of your Savior as long as you live. How? By studying God's Word, by obeying His commandments, and by allowing His Son to reign over your heart.

Are you seeking to become a more mature believer? Hopefully so, because that's exactly what God wants you to become . . . and it's exactly what you should want to become, too!

Thoughts for Today

I've never met anyone who became instantly
mature. It's a painstaking process that
God takes us through, and it includes such
things as waiting, failing, losing, and
being misunderstood—each calling for
extra doses of perseverance.
Charles Swindoll

Salvation is not an event; it is a process.
Henry Blackaby

Having a doctrine pass before the mind is not
what the Bible means by knowing the truth.
It's only when it reaches down deep into
the heart that the truth begins to set us free,
just as a key must penetrate a lock to turn it,
or as rainfall must saturate the earth down to
the roots in order for your garden to grow.
John Eldredge

his devotional

A Tip for Today

Obedience Leads to Spiritual Growth:
Oswald Sanders correctly observed,
"We grow spiritually as our Lord grew
physically: by a life of simple,
unobtrusive obedience."

A Prayer for Today

Lord, help me to keep growing
spiritually and emotionally.
Let me live according to
Your Word, and let me grow
in my faith every day that
I live. Amen

Loving God... with All Your Heart

Love the LORD your God with all your heart and with all your soul and with all your strength.

Deuteronomy 6:5 NIV

C. S. Lewis observed, "A man's spiritual health is exactly proportional to his love for God." If we are to enjoy the spiritual health that God intends for us, we must praise Him, we must love Him, and we must obey Him.

When we worship God faithfully and obediently, we invite His love into our hearts. When we truly worship God, we allow Him to rule over our days and our lives. In turn, we grow to love God *even more* deeply as we sense His love for us.

St. Augustine wrote, "I love you, Lord, not doubtingly, but with absolute certainty. Your Word beat upon my heart until I fell in love with you, and now the universe and everything in it tells me to love you."

Today, open your heart to the Father. And let your obedience be a fitting response to His never-ending love.

Thoughts for Today

What is Christian perfection? Loving God
with all our heart, mind, soul, and strength.
John Wesley

The only way to love God with all our soul
is to give up our lives for His sake.
Oswald Chambers

The church has no greater need today than to
fall in love with Jesus all over again.
Vance Havner

Everything in your Christian life, everything
about knowing Him and experiencing Him,
everything about knowing His will,
depends on the quality of your
love relationship to God.
Henry Blackaby

his devotional

A Tip for Today

Express Yourself . . .
If you sincerely love God, don't be bashful
to tell Him so. And while you're at it,
don't be bashful to tell other people about
your feelings. If you love God, say so!

A Prayer for Today

Dear Heavenly Father, You have blessed me
with a love that is infinite and eternal. Let me
love You, Lord, more and more each day.
Make me a loving servant, Father, today and
throughout eternity. And, let me show my love
for You by sharing Your message and
Your love with others. Amen

Walkin' with the Son

As you therefore have received Christ Jesus the Lord,
so walk in Him, having been firmly rooted and
now being built up in Him and established in your faith,
just as you were instructed, and overflowing with gratitude.

Colossians 2:6, 7 NASB

Are you tired? Discouraged? Fearful? Be comforted. And take a walk with God.

The 19th-century writer Hannah Whitall Smith observed, "The crucial question for each of us is this: What do you think of Jesus, and do you yet have a personal acquaintance with Him?" Indeed, the answer to that question will determine the quality, the course, and the direction of your life today *and* for all eternity.

Jesus has called upon believers of every generation (and that includes you) to walk with Him. Jesus promises that when you follow in His footsteps, He will teach you how to live freely and lightly (Matthew 11:28-30). And when Jesus makes a promise, you can depend upon it.

Are you worried or anxious? Be confident in God's power. He will never desert you. Do you see no hope for the future? Be courageous and call upon God. He will protect you and then use you according to His purposes. Are

you confused? Listen to the quiet voice of your
Heavenly Father. He is not a God of confusion.
Talk with Him; listen to Him; walk with Him;
follow His commandments. He is steadfast,
and He is your Protector . . . forever.

Thoughts for Today

If you walk with the Lord,
you'll never be out of step.
Anonymous

Teach a man a rule and you help him solve
a problem; teach a man to walk with God and
you help him solve the rest of his life.
John Eldredge

I would rather walk with God in the dark
than go alone in the light.
Anonymous

A Tip for Today

If You Want to Be a Disciple of Christ . . .
follow in His footsteps, obey
His commandments, and
share His never-ending love.

A Prayer for Today

Dear Lord, each day I need to walk
with You. Your presence provides
me security and comfort. As we walk
together, Lord, may Your Presence
be reflected in my life, and may
Your love dwell within my heart . Amen

More Good Stuff from the Good Book

Bible Verses by Topic

Anger

Whosoever is angry with his brother without a cause shall be in danger of the judgment....
Matthew 5:22 KJV

Patient people have great understanding, but people with quick tempers show their foolishness.
Proverbs 14:29 NCV

A gentle answer turns away wrath, but a harsh word stirs up anger.
Proverbs 15:1 NIV

Do not let the sun go down on your anger, and do not give the devil an opportunity.
Ephesians 4:26, 27 NASB

Stop your anger!
Turn from your rage!
Do not envy others—
it only leads to harm.

Psalm 37:8 NLT

Integrity

A good name is more desirable than
great riches; to be esteemed is better
than silver or gold.
Proverbs 22:1 NIV

We also rejoice in our sufferings, because we
know that suffering produces perseverance;
perseverance, character; and character, hope.
Romans 5:3, 4 NIV

In everything set them an example by doing
what is good. In your teaching show integrity,
seriousness and soundness of speech that
cannot be condemned, so that those who
oppose you may be ashamed because
they have nothing bad to say about us.
Titus 2:7 NIV

Your Problems and God's Solutions

Let not your heart be troubled:
ye believe in God, believe also in me.
John 14:1 KJV

I have told you these things, so that in me
you may have peace. In this world
you will have trouble. But take heart!
I have overcome the world.
John 16:33 NIV

LORD, help! they cried in their trouble, and he
saved them from their distress.
Psalm 107:13 NLT

Thanksgiving and Thanksliving

And let the peace of God rule in your hearts,
to which also you were called in one body;
and be thankful.
Colossians 3:15 NKJV

You are my God, and I will give you thanks;
you are my God, and I will exalt you.
Give thanks to the LORD, for he is good;
his love endures forever.
Psalm 118:28,29 NIV

Be cheerful no matter what; pray all the time;
thank God no matter what happens.
This is the way God wants you
who belong to Christ Jesus to live.
1 Thessalonians 5:16-18 MSG

Christ's Love

We love Him because He first loved us.
1 John 4:19 NKJV

Now return to the LORD your God,
For He is gracious and compassionate,
Slow to anger, abounding in lovingkindness.
Joel 2:13 NASB

The unfailing love of the Lord never ends!
Lamentations 3:22 NLT

The LORD's unfailing love surrounds
the man who trusts in him.
Psalm 32:10 NIV

Strength for Today

I will give you a new heart
and put a new spirit in you….
Ezekiel 36:26 NIV

The Lord says, "Forget what happened before,
and do not think about the past. Look at
the new thing I am going to do. It is already
happening. Don't you see it? I will make
a road in the desert and rivers in the dry land.
Isaiah 43:18, 19 NCV

For though a righteous man falls seven times,
he rises again….
Proverbs 24:16 NIV

Therefore if anyone is in Christ,
he is a new creature;
the old things passed away;
behold, new things have come.

2 Corinthians 5:17 HCSB

Forgiveness

Do not judge, and you will not be judged.
Do not condemn, and you will not
be condemned. Forgive, and
you will be forgiven.
Luke 6:37 HCSB

And whenever you stand praying,
if you have anything against anyone,
forgive him, so that your Father in heaven
may also forgive you your wrongdoing.
Mark 11:25 HCSB

Then Peter came to him and asked,
"Lord, how often should I forgive someone
who sins against me? Seven times?" "No!"
Jesus replied, "seventy times seven!"
Matthew 18:21, 22 NLT

Courage

I can do all things through Him
who strengthens me.
Philippians 4:13 NASB

Depend on the Lord and his strength;
always go to him for help.
Remember the miracles he has done;
remember his wonders and his decisions.
Psalm 105:4, 5 NCV

I will lift up my eyes to the hills—From whence
comes my help? My help comes from the Lord,
Who made heaven and earth.
Psalm 121:1, 2 NKJV

God is our refuge and strength,
a very present help in trouble.
Psalm 46:1 NKJV

Faith

The righteous will live by his faith.
Habakkuk 2:4 NIV

Have faith in the LORD your God
and you will be upheld.
2 Chronicles 20:20 NIV

I have fought the good fight,
I have finished the race, I have kept the faith.
2 Timothy 4:7 NIV

Faith without works is dead.
James 2:20 KJV

Perseverance

Consider it pure joy, my brothers,
whenever you face trials of many kinds,
because you know that the testing of
your faith develops perseverance.
James 1:2, 3 NIV

Patient endurance is what you need now,
so you will continue to do God's will.
Then you will receive all that he has promised.
Hebrews 10:36 NLT

Let us not become weary in doing good,
for at the proper time we will reap
a harvest if we do not give up.
Galatians 6:9 NIV

We are hard pressed on every side,
yet not crushed; we are perplexed,
but not in despair.
2 Corinthians 4:8 NKJV

Facing Our Fears

But He said to them, "Why are you fearful,
you of little faith?" Then He got up and
rebuked the winds and the sea.
And there was a great calm.
Matthew 8:26 HCSB

Fear of man will prove to be a snare, but
whoever trusts in the LORD is kept safe.
Proverbs 29:25 NIV

The Lord is my light and my salvation—
so why should I be afraid? The Lord protects
me from danger—so why should I tremble?
Psalm 27:1 NLT

Cast your burden upon the Lord and
He will sustain you: He will never allow
the righteous to be shaken.
Psalm 55:22 NASB

Be of good courage,
And He shall
strengthen your heart,
All you who hope in
the Lord.

Psalm 31:24 NKJV

Living in the Present

Give your entire attention to what God
is doing right now, and don't get worked
up about what may or may not happen
tomorrow. God will help you deal
with whatever hard things come up when
the time comes.
Matthew 6:34 MSG

This is the day which the LORD has made;
let us rejoice and be glad in it.
Psalm 118:24 NASB

For he says, "In the time of my favor I heard
you, and in the day of salvation I helped you."
I tell you, now is the time of God's favor,
now is the day of salvation.
2 Corinthians 6:2 NIV

Living on Purpose

To everything there is a season,
a time for every purpose under heaven.
Ecclesiastes 3:1 NKJV

You will show me the path of life;
in Your presence is fullness of joy;
at Your right hand are pleasures forevermore.
Psalm 16:11 NKJV

May He grant you according to your
heart's desire, and fulfill all your purpose.
Psalm 20:4 NKJV

We know that all things work together for
the good of those who love God: those who
are called according to His purpose.
Romans 8:28 HCSB

Praise

At the name of Jesus every knee should bow,
of those in heaven, and of those on earth,
and of those under the earth, and that every
tongue should confess that Jesus Christ is
Lord, to the glory of God the Father.
Philippians 2:10, 11 NKJV

Is anyone happy? Let him sing songs of praise.
James 5:13 NIV

Through Him then, let us continually offer up
a sacrifice of praise to God, that is,
the fruit of lips that give thanks to His name.
Hebrews 13:15 NASB

Great is the Lord, and greatly to be praised;
And His greatness is unsearchable.
Psalm 145:3 NKJV

But as for me,
I will **always**
have **hope**;
I will **praise** you
more and more.

Psalm 71:14 NIV

Acts of Kindness

This is what the LORD Almighty says:
Judge fairly and honestly, and show mercy
and kindness to one another.
Zechariah 7:9 NLT

Be kindly affectionate to one another with
brotherly love, in honor giving preference to
one another; not lagging in diligence,
fervent in spirit, serving the Lord;
rejoicing in hope, patient in tribulation,
continuing steadfastly in prayer.
Romans 12:10-12 NKJV

Kind words are like honey—
sweet to the soul and healthy for the body.
Proverbs 16:24 NLT

Be kind to each other,
tenderhearted,
forgiving one another,
just as God through Christ
has forgiven you.

Ephesians 4:32 NLT